Books by Lois Wyse

LOVETALK

HOW TO SAY WHAT YOU MEAN
TO SOMEONE YOU LOVE

LOVETALK

HOW TO SAY WHAT YOU MEAN TO SOMEONE YOU LOVE

LOIS WYSE

DOUBLEDAY & COMPANY, INC., GARDEN CITY, NEW YORK

1973

ISBN: 0-385-07421-2
Library of Congress Catalog Card Number 73–79729
Copyright © 1973 by Lois Wyse
All Rights Reserved
Printed in the United States of America

I really do not know just when or how
I began to write these pages.
They are a record of my experiences,
Many of which I did not fully understand
Until I saw them written.

I guess I started out looking for
Small signs on the road.
I ended with
A basic philosophy of love,
A new awareness of us.

I do not know if everyone
Has faced my particular crises.
(I always think I must be the only one.
Until I wrote that first book of love poetry,
I thought no one else had ever had those feelings.)

But this I do know now:
The first part of my life
Taught me how to live
The rest of my life.
And for the rest of my life I will love you.

LOVETALK

HOW TO SAY WHAT YOU MEAN
TO SOMEONE YOU LOVE

1

There are no authorities on love
The way there are on, say . . .

                 tropical fish or eighteenth-century literature.
And I don't know any more about love
              than the average lady who loves.
Nobody knows exactly when love begins,
Precisely how it ends,
And why, at midpoint, it curves more wildly
            than a woman pumped to her prime by silicone.

There have been times I have not recognized love
Until it was too late to do anything about it.

I suppose that has happened to others, too, and they never know until
He dies.
Or she marries a sales manager in Akron, Ohio.

Maybe that is why some of us
In a miasma composed of lost loves and old Kleenex
haunt museums
and libraries
and arty film houses
Wearing our old loves as an excuse for our present lives.

For some of us
The pretend world is easier to live in than the real world,
For in that twilight of ill-discerned shapes and answers

We move the partners in our affections
According to our will to win them.

In real life
You and I have found that loves won once are not necessarily won
Forever.

The will to win is not everything.
That is what Hollywood never taught us.
In old-style films everybody lived happily everafter,
But I know girls who got divorced right after the ceremony,
And we know some couples who never really have been married,
And look at all the ones who after ten or twenty years have called it
Quits.

So who's at fault?
Is it us or the movies?

I mean, after all, if Lana Turner could make it
Against such terrible odds in film after film,
Doesn't that mean there is something wrong with me
When I fail to cope with a husband who doesn't talk
            and children who do not listen?

On second thought
Maybe there is something wrong with the old movies.
Maybe we are the ones who are normal
(Whatever that means).
Of course, normal is not only indefinable but varying.
What is normal for me may be absolutely unthinkable to you
(On second thought . . . not unthinkable . . . just dumb or
                            irrelevant or wrong).
But who is to say what is wrong?

Who is to say what is right?
Almost everybody. In this society of differing values
All of us seem to put a premium on love.
We hang Sister Corita posters in our offices
And plaster peace symbols on our rear windows.
We speak kindly of children who live together
(While praying that ours do not so indulge themselves)
And we start and end each of these love-filled days
In a home where love may never, ever be mentioned.

Is this what love is all about?
Is it a press agent's version of Love in America?
Is love a *thing*
Or *the* thing
That moves our lives?
Are we accommodating life to love or love to life
And which is better?
You know something?
I really don't think it's much different at country clubs than
            it is at communes.

There is a lot of talk about love
And not much love.
Maybe we should stop talking so much about love in the third person
And try it oftener in the first person.
Maybe what we really need is
Lovetalk.

I

Underneath the surface courtesy in all our lives
There is an enormous amount of hate, anger, frustration, and
                disappointment.
Seething inside is a bitterness we cannot smile away.
We really want to get rid of those things we call
Irish miseries, German pride, English reserve, Latin temperament,
                Scotch thrift, Jewish possessiveness
And give ourselves totally to a kind of warm, international
                loving feeling.

The problem is, my dear, I can acknowledge my ethnic faults
. . . oh, I am very good at assuming blame . . .
That old Puritan ethic of self-blame bends my back, bows my head;
But how good am I at acknowledging my need to give and get
Lovetalk?

I am an expert in Smalltalk.
I walk through life and play the roles for
Teachertalk, Parenttalk, Studenttalk, Employertalk, and
                                        Employeetalk.
But no one ever told me in real words
(as opposed to unreal words like the lyrics you sing
                and the poems we recite in bed together)
No one ever told me in real words

How to put
Lovetalk
Into my life with the same frequency as coffee, tea, and milk.

But then no one has really defined
Lovetalk.
So I think I'll be the one.

Definition:
Lovetalk
Is what I say to you
And what you say to me
That warms me even when I don't have any right to feel warm.
Lovetalk
Is the conversation
That takes on its particular colorings
Because of the participants,
The time,
The place,
The tone,
The circumstance.
The subject is incidental.

Lovetalk.
That nice little talk that happens in bed before we go to sleep.
Lovetalk.
The look you give me when you think no one is looking.
Lovetalk.
The book I buy for you when you least expect a present.
Lovetalk.
The thing that must happen so love can happen.
Lovetalk
With you is what makes it easier for me to avoid meantalk with others.

Lovetalk
Is the key to feeling good.

It is why I don't need
Uppers and downers, a macrobiotic diet,
And a faithful reading of my horoscope.

The problem is that I make
Lovetalk
Sporadically.
Lovetalk,
To be effective, must be constant.
But who shows us how to make continual Lovetalk?
Baedeker never wrote a guide, and Standard Oil doesn't give maps.

Where and how do we learn about love?

Certainly not in our public, private, or parochial schools.
We pay taxes and sometimes tuition
To support educational systems where we teach everything
Except love and the ways to express it.
We Teach water-skiing and archery,
Political science and the humanities.
We have a course and book for every subject,
But the closest we get to love
Is to debate the wisdom of sex-education programs.
We nod appreciatively when we are told about cooking classes.
We expect children to learn about friendship from our example
And from teachers who put students in work/friend situations.
We encourage our children to be athletic.

> "Throw the ball to Daddy"
> "You're six, Timmy. It's time you learned to ride a bike."
> "Of course she'll take swimming lessons."

And we lecture kids with great passion on the need to
Respect the right of others.

       "That's Mary's ball. Give it back to her."
       "Tom is your guest; let him have chocolate."
       "Blacks and whites are equal."
But who teaches our children . . . and who taught us . . .
How to love?

There are a zillion how-to sex books,
         but most of us forget that sex never was and never will
         be a synonym for love. I have always liked the Rollo
         May differentiation in which sex is defined as stimulus
         and response, while love is a state of being. But who
         instructs us in the geography of that state of being?

2

I remember how I met you.
I guess everybody who loves somebody remembers how they met.
I remember the first time I saw you.
That is the key word:
Saw.
I saw you.
Love starts with a look,
A meeting of the eyes that locks two people in understanding.
I melted. Just a little. Not so anyone could notice.
From then on there was excitement,
Anticipation for the next meeting
And before long I had propelled me into deeper emotional waters.
Non-verbal.
The whole thing was non-verbal.

But could I have continued to fantasize
If we had never talked?

Many people distrust words, and for good reason.
We have all been deceived by words.
We have all failed at some time
To say precisely what we meant because
We could not find the proper words.
How many times have I shrugged my shoulders,
Smiled sheepishly, and said,
Oh, you know what I mean.

But do you?
I mean if you don't really know what is in my head
When I can't express
Dum dum things like going to the store or hanging a shelf,
How are you supposed to know what I mean when
I talk about things we cannot see?

Lovetalk?
When does the
Lovetalk
Begin?

I do not know precisely.
The man-woman relationship is sometimes so hard to come by
That we usually never know when it all began or
                    just how or when or why we lose it.

I think we begin to lose
Love
The day the
Lovetalk
Stops.
But for some
The Lovetalk never starts.

How can the
Lovetalk
Start
When we are so tongue-tied
By convention and inadequate vocabulary?
How can the
Lovetalk
Start
When we are running after planes and children and overdue loans?

I guess we have to make it happen.
I do not really believe in miracles,
And you must know by now that I am not a fatalist.

I believe that we make good things happen in our lives
And, if we try hard, we can keep some bad things away.
So if we can take the time to live,
Can we not take the time to love?

And can't
Lovetalk
Become an adjunct of love?

3

Lovetalk is not a one-night stand
Or a one-night change
From Nothing
To Something.

I think
Lovetalk
Has to start in me.

Doesn't that sound rather strange
Considering the twoness of love itself?
And if it starts with just me,
Then it must begin with self-dialogue.

I learned about self-dialogue from you.
I think it was the summer we had all those heat waves.
Yes. That is when it was.
You told me that if people communicated with themselves
            before they spoke to others,
They would stop talking about the damned, boring weather.
And I asked you how to do it.
So you told me about self-dialogue.
            Me talking to me.
It is hard to talk to me.
Where do I start my dialogue, self-dialogue, of Lovetalk?

Questions. I keep asking questions.
Of course. That is it. I start Lovetalk with questions.
Self-questioning. Self-questioning seems so selfish.

> But it is results that count.
> The results are not selfish.
> The result is a healthier Us.

I have been playing at self-dialogue a few years now.
I know the best times:

> In the shower or tub.

There is something about physical nakedness
> that lets me bare my thoughts.
When I am out of clothes and feel the steamy, soapy, perfumed
> atmosphere, my thoughts are all released.
They are coming now.

Steamy, soapy questions.

> What do I need?
> What do I really want?
> Will a new dress cover my hurts?
> Can another house shelter my desires?
> Do I want to go slower?
> Faster?
> Do I want more times together?
> Or more time alone?
> What is it that I really need?

I bounce the questions from one part of me to another.
I roll the questions in my mouth.
I scrub my back with them,
Sometimes saying answers above the sound of running water.
I listen. My voice anchors me to reality.
I touch the answers with my heart,
Feel them with my hands.
It may take a year or two until

The answers become a part of me,
But each day I will work a little harder.
I will not always come a little closer.

The steam is evaporating now,
And I used up all the soap.

*

It is a long time now between steamy, soapy showers.

I am less concerned with questions than with answers.
I am beginning to come up with answers.
They are filed near the front of my mind.
I am waiting to bring them out in the open.
No no no no.
This is not best friend talk.
I cannot even discuss these things with you.
You could be hurt by my indecision. You could be concerned.
You could change toward me. No. These questions are not for you.
Yet I must see them openly.
So I take paper and pencil.
I am ready to make a list of the needs I suspect are deepest,
Most relevant to my finding love by speaking love.

Now I put on paper the answers, the needs I have so long discussed with me. Now I put in writing the words that say precisely what I mean. No almost words. No namby-pamby, watered-down thoughts. These are to be exact words. Maybe the answers are highly emotional; maybe they look prejudiced on paper. So be it. I am allowed to be emotional at this time; no one is asking for cool appraisals. The key thing now is to know that what I have written honestly reflects my opinions about my own needs. There is no deadline on this project. I will take the time I require to put my thoughts in perspective. I will write my list of needs in the order that I feel them. Then I will put the list away. A week later I will see if it still says what I mean.

Good week. Surprising. I did not expect a good week. It is a relief to make the list. Like walking out of class after a tough exam. OK. So I will look at the list. In the pantyhose drawer. What could be less suspect? Oh. I cringe when I read the list. What do I mean by flat, overstated phrases like, "I want privacy," and "I need time." A month from now I will read it all again. Meanwhile I will rewrite rewrite simplify simplify.

It is not a month later. It is seven months later. I guess I am a slow thinker. But now I can read the list without cringing. I no longer embarrass me. I am ready for the second step. I am ready to make a list of your needs.

＊

Your list is easier to write than mine, because I do not know you as well as I know me. Even though you have been a part of my life for the past hundred years, I do not know you totally. That is good. I do not want to. I do not really know how complex you are. I do not know all the temptations, the wildness, the small glints of netherworld that flash unsuspected against the safety of your everydayness. So I guess. I take calculated chances in determining your needs. One caution to myself: I must not write a list of needs I think you should have. I must write a list of needs I think you do have. Even if I do not approve of them. I will not be a judge, just a reporter. The editorials can come later.

＊

I have done it. It really was not difficult. I am the hard one; you are easy. I sit at my desk, and the little Tensor lamp shines on you and me. You and me lists. Now I can go further. I can begin on us.

＊

An us is a separate person. An us is not a combination of you and me. An us is a creature we invent from those things two people take from themselves as individuals.

＊

I want to be part of The Harmonious Us.

The Harmonious Us
Is not the figment of our imagination.

The Harmonious Us
Is the reality of our imagination.

4

The thought of building
The Harmonious Us
Is scary.
I mean I really do have some fears.

But let me go back to my basic premise:
Lovetalk means verbalize.
Verbalize, speak, say, bring forth the fears.

I am afraid to say too much.

I have other fears. About a million.

I will confine them to the fears in creating
The Harmonious Us.
There are 13 fears.
Unlucky number?
Lucky number?
Luck or no, the number is 13.

Even my fears are spooky. OK, here goes.

FEAR LIST:

1) How much can I confide to you?
2) Can I really say all the things I want about my family?
3) Your family?
4) Your co-workers?
5) My friends?
6) At what point will my confessions make you uneasy about me?
7) At what point will I turn you off instead of helping you to understand us?
8) How much can I say about the way I feel for you?
9) How deeply can I afford to describe my needs before you back away in fear that you cannot fulfill them?
10) Will you be revulsed by my needs?
11) At what point and how do I get you to talk, to say the things you think, to talk about your dreams, your needs, your reactions?
12) How do I get you to probe deeper than you ever have, so that you become dizzy with self-knowledge, yet still recognize that it is our love that brought it out?
13) How do I touch the hidden parts of you and bring to light for both of us those unique parts of you?

I just reread it.
It is not such a forbidding, foreboding list, after all.

I have thought a lot about my fears.
I gave up *Time* and *Newsweek*
And I have not seen television for over a week.

Television.
So many television marriages.
How do we avoid a television marriage,
That playing out of lives against the background of the tube?
Instead of our two lives filling the room,
There are *their* two lives and the eleven o'clock news with
Constant commercial interruptions.
Instead of what you say and what I say,
It is what Dick and Johnny and their guests say.
You don't laugh with me;
I don't laugh with you.
All the wit comes pouring out of the tube,
And we laugh at it together.
The more we avoid talking,
The more passive the relationship becomes.
Television permits us to walk through life
With minor speaking parts.
There is so much talk coming at us all day and all night
That we sit in quiet relief because we do not have to speak.
And the more we fail to speak,
The more difficult speaking becomes.
We push everything deeper and deeper into
Some small, dark part of ourselves.
We stuff it deeper and deeper and deeper.
It becomes so dark and deep we forget it until
It comes back to haunt us in our dreams the nights we sleep
And in our turning-tossing wakefulness the nights we don't.

We treat our love with diffidence.
We are afraid to say the three most important love words of all:
I need you.

Only those needs that can be expressed can be answered,
And of all human needs,
The greatest is love.

I need you.
I need you.
There. I said it.
Turn off the tube, please.
I need you.

I need us.

Everybody needs an Us.
Everybody.
Everybody.
Everybody.

Even you.

5

They are really an adorable couple,
And they live together just because they like living together.
You know, they're not together because it's cheaper
Or he liked her Dali prints and she liked his Princess telephone.
They just like living together.
It's kind of sweet really.
They're old enough to mean it and young enough to enjoy it.
I guess they're in their late twenties.
Anyway, I liked them immediately. They each have good jobs,
And they talk about them appealingly.

But about ten minutes after I met them
I knew the whole situation was crummy.
I mean this wasn't any of that mutually-satisfying garbage.
It was OK for him, but inside the girl was dying.
She wanted to get married.

The next time I saw the fellow I asked him why he didn't marry her.
Look, I said, are you going to keep playing house until you're 90?
He wrinkled his forehead, sighed, and said that
He didn't want to be tied down.
He wanted to be free.

When he said that, I guess he expected me to shout
Bravo, huzzah, and hooray.
But you know something? It made me sick.
Who is he to say that marriage isn't for free people?

I didn't say anything to him. I didn't communicate.
I didn't use Lovetalk. I didn't stop to think that Lovetalk isn't
Just for the one person you love.
Lovetalk is for everyday for everyone.

Why didn't I say to him that
A good marriage frees people; it does not enslave them.
I really believe that.
In a good marriage the ability to communicate
And to express fears and hopes
(the two things that are most difficult to express)
Makes it possible for us to act freely and gain the understanding
                of our partner.
The enslaved man or woman
Is the one who cannot express fears or hopes and therefore
Stays in intolerable situations.

That's Lovetalk.
I must use it more often.
Maybe if I can get back to
The Harmonious Us
I will get closer to
Lovetalk
All the time.

Most of us don't get what we want in life.
Remember John Guare's play *The House of Blue Leaves*
With the zookeeper who is kept alive by his fantasies?
Crazy nutsy fantasies about movie stars and Kennedys and the Pope?
Well, I'm not trying to say it's like that with everybody.
But in some ways it is.
We all dream dreams, and precious few of them materialize.
We don't get what we want in life,
And we don't get what we want in love.
But we have more freedom to change things in love
Than we do in life.

We really can change the love we give and get,
And the potential for full love is truly in our hands.
Love is not the exclusive property of the young; they just think it is.
There is the greening of love,
The blooming of love,
And the ripening of love.
But none of these stages is static,
And we can slide forward, backward, or even slip sideways
In this growing and waning relationship we call
Love.

Because of this constant change
Even old marriages
Like ours
Can be revitalized in brief encounters with highly charged love.
Maybe I should say . . . especially old marriages . . .
Because unlike those who are afraid to marry
We have made a commitment to love and to life.

How can we help our old love?

The most exhilarating fantasizing
Is when a single couple pretends they are married
And a married couple pretends they are single.

Sometimes we tell each other stories,
Stories we make up.
Regular "once upon a time" stories.
We call it inventing love.

Evelyn read one of those Hollywood lingerie
catalogues and ordered a leopard print nightgown.
She didn't tell Henry. It was to be their anniversary
surprise. The night of their anniversary she put on
eyeliner and sparkle face powder and perfume. Then
she slithered into the leopard nightgown. Henry
walked into the bedroom, sniffed the perfumed
bedchamber, looked at her, and roared with laughter.
"Which one are you?" he guffawed, "Tarzan or
Jane?" Henry thought it was such a funny scene that
he told the story to all their friends. Two years later
she got the divorce.

Rule One: Never laugh at the fantasies
of someone you love.
Rule Two: Should you break Rule One,
never tell a living soul.

Fantasizing is not for women only.

You can fantasize things into reality.
For instance, you can dream about a perfect afternoon
And then make it happen for both of us.

The best way to start fantasizing is
With two words . . . I wish . . .
Just say . . . I wish . . .
And it is very surprising
How many wishes
I will make come true for you.
And if you ask me to make a wish
That you can make come true
You will have proven love exists
And so caused new blessings to come to
The Harmonious Us.

My friend who lived with the pretty lady fantasized all wrong. He kept thinking about situations that hurt his love.

How can love grow if he saturates it with doubt and misgivings?

In what ways would marriage restrict him and make him less human?

How can a girl you've lived with, and been faithful to, for two years tie you up in ways she already hasn't?

I wonder if he ever asked her. Maybe if he did he would learn some things about himself. Maybe he would learn what he expected of himself . . . really.

Maybe I should ask you more questions.
I want to get back to The Harmonious Us.
I miss Us.
You have been away three days.
I can stand being away from you.
It is Us that I miss most.

Do you think if my friend fantasizes good instead of bad he can relax and enchant and delight Them?

Someday . . . oh, maybe two girls from now . . . he'll find out, if she is tying him down or if he is tying him down. Somehow I think . . . you know what I think . . . I think he is the one who is not loosening the tight bonds he puts on himself.

Hey, fellow, you're cutting love off at the pass.

Why don't you just take a deep breath and say, "With all the freedom in the world . . . this is what I would do. . . ."

If you had all the freedom, what would you do? Would you still choose me? Don't answer that. I'll fantasize a response. That will be good for The Harmonious Us.

I think The Harmonious Us is often aided by questions I do not ask.

I begin to understand The Harmonious Us when I take a piece of paper (verbalizing is not enough; somehow we must see the words in writing) and write the qualities I seek in The Harmonious Us.

I call the list The Top Ten.

Look, everything I do isn't brilliant.

But it says what I mean. I really mean that these are the qualities I want in The Harmonious Us.

6

New chapter. New day. New world. New life.
What's new? Us. That's what's new. How's that for openers?
OK, down to business.
The List.
You have to understand, and I guess you do,
That The Harmonious Us
Does not have to have my individual qualities
Or your individual qualities
In order to have our individual qualities.
The Harmonious Us
Is what we want this new personality, The Us, to be.
These, then, are the best of us:
1. Peace   2. Stimulation
3. Earthiness   4. Sense of the sublime
5. Sense of belonging   6. Freedom
7. Beauty   8. Disregard for the physical
9. Memory of the past   10. Anticipation of the future

Understand the list?
Look, my love. It works in pairs. Like us.

One and two go together.
Three and four.
Five and six.
Seven and eight.
Nine and ten.

They are absolute opposites. Dichotomies.
My friend John says
Growth comes through the balance of opposites.
Look, John, The Harmonious Us comes about the same way.
Corollary: The Harmonious Us is growth.

Come grow with me, my love.

One and two. Peace and Stimulation.

Opposites.
Dum dum.
Swing it one way, look at it another.
I want to find peace in Us,
But Us must still exhilarate me.
What do I mean by peace?
Comfort. Acceptance.
In Us I want to be free to be me
Without lipstick.
   Relax.
    Sigh.
    Unwind
long enough to burrow deep and find
The challenge that keeps me alive.
I do not really want a sedentary life.
I want to dip into Us
And sip the cool water before I go back to the boiling kettle.
I still want the heat.
Bubble bubble.
Yet I need the acceptance.
I want to be consoled by Us when the fires go out.

Help me. Help me. I cannot make the pot boil just now. Hold back
the world a little while. Make it wait. Help me. Hold Us close.

Three and Four. Earthiness/Sense of the Sublime

I must be careful not to make my life
A one-character play . . .
So busy writing my history
I fail to live it.
Where are the relationships?
Where is the impact of others on my life?
I root myself in humdrum earthiness
        brush teeth go to work smile eat
But are roots enough?

I must flower, too.
I must push out of the dirt that covers me and reach for
The sun that warms me,
Be exposed to the rain that is inevitable
For my growth.
But the roots   the earthiness   the bed
must be there. I must push up from
                                something.

But of what are my roots made?
Chance?
More and more I think so.
I cannot choose
The quality of roots.

I can only direct
The flowering.

                        How does my garden grow?
                        By doing first the things I must.

So much symbolism
For such a little life.

Five and Six. Sense of Belonging/Freedom

I must watch myself
Because in my need to belong
I can be shortchanged.
I can say too much
For joy that is short-lived
And wait too long
For days that do not come.
I must learn to set the prices
That are fair to me
So that there may be a just Us
For Just Us.

I find it easier to give freedom
Than to take it.
So many decisions to make when one is free.
Choice is the burden of freedom,
And wrong choice is the price.

If I could but balance
These schizoid qualities
I would lose myself in love
And find myself in Us.

I want to turn to Us for comfort,
But I don't want to stop being me
Or have you give up
Those unique qualities
That made you so appealing
The first time around.

Let's lean lightly.

Ping
    ping
Delicate footwork
This balancing act.

Seven and Eight. Beauty/Disregard for the Physical

Flowers in ev'ry room in my head,
White wine in paper-thin crystal.
I want to walk in beauty
With the swaying, tender spirits
That fill my life with joy.

Love is supposed to be a thing apart
From the things that money can buy,
But I do not know why
Love cannot work its wonders
In a house where china matches.
Who is to say that love is for those
Who can keep warm no other way?

   When times are good,
    love can be good, too,
   So long as I do not make the presence of beauty
    a reason for giving love,
   Or the absence of beauty
    an excuse for giving more
     than you have any right to take.

My love must be given
Because my love must be given.

Nine and Ten. Memory of Past/Anticipation of Future

Past enchantments blind me
Like a mirror held to sunlight;
And my dreams distort the future
Like a mirror cracked with use.

Oh, let my mem'ry serve me well,
Let not hope outshine the truth,
For we must weave the past and future
Into the here and now of Us.

All right, so I know what I need in
The Harmonious Us.
Now how can I breathe it into being?

An Us does not begin in the womb.
It is gentled into life through the head and the heart.
This I know.
So we must talk . . .
Lovetalk . . .
The Harmonious Us
Into continual being, for Lovetalk does not end with this semester.

Lovetalk is lifelong.

       We cannot live a life
             that does not speak.
       We cannot live a life
             that alarms itself to waking,
             lunches itself,
             drives itself to dinner . . .
             and so to bed.

Such a life is depressing.
And I know now what depression is.
Depression is
That aging of the spirit

That begins with lack of Lovetalk
And ends with lack of love.

＊

No love.

No links.

No wonder
we must save us now.

But how?
How do we talk
The Harmonious Us
Into life?

How do we speak of Us
And to Us?

What is the best kind of
Lovetalk
For Us?

Starting Place:
A point of mutual agreement.
Like or dislike; doesn't matter
Just so long as we begin someplace
Where we both nod yes.

Doesn't matter if it's
Red China
Black dresses
Or purple people.

If we agree, let's talk.
In between I will slip the message in . . .

I'm glad you're home today.
I think you are very smart.
I am proud of you.
Let's do something together, just the two of us,
                              Saturday afternoon.
Somewhere between China and the black hem,
I will take little stitches to outline the pattern of our love.

So goes Lovetalk.
So grows Lovetalk

Out of satisfactions
That we list,
Out of needs
That we express.

The heart of our love:
Satisfaction and need,
The blending of the two.

Strange.
They are also
Opposites.

Balance the opposites.
Balance need and satisfaction
To get Lovetalk.

To reach the satisfactions
We must understand the needs
And put a ceiling on them,
For in my quest for love
I could give the essence of my spirit:
                    My self-respect
                    My independence.

These are too much to give for love.

Yet how do we keep giving year after year?
I know that in a long-time relationship
We can become quite bored
With the cadence of each other's speech,
The predictable questions,
The same answers,
The itches and scratches.

We need new thoughts,
New stimulations
Or we will become
Echoes of our former selves.

Such a delicate bridge to cross.
Verbalization requires the most delicate balance of all.

Talk talk overtalk
Is love's overkill.

But ummm . . . uhhh . . .
Undertalk
Is love's frustration.
Slow starvation.

Undertalk
Means love cannot feed itself
And will ultimately die of lack of nourishment.

So, my dear, we must nourish love
With talk sweet talk
Lovetalk
That we share.

Thoughts.
All thoughts.
Just thoughts.

The hardest part of Lovetalk
        is in the receiving, not the giving.
        For the one who makes Lovetalk,
        the emotions are as well ordered
        as a grocery list: a pint of need,
        two bunches of red compliments.

To listen to Lovetalk
        requires a special frame of mind,
        and it is not easy to throw off
        the cares of check writing and
        silver polishing to bring to high glow
        those inner parts of us that
        are tarnished with disuse.

Listen. Listen
        for the unspoken sounds of love.

An apple when you did not ask for one.

A kiss in the morning. A kiss at night.

A kiss when no one is looking.

A kiss when someone is looking.

A fire in the fireplace.

A freshly shaven face.

The worry lines that come from children-watching.

7

In every good love there are bad times.
There are times when love becomes
A burden. A duty. An obligation.
There comes the day when you first know
That it will not always be constant joy.
The first reaction is to end this love
And find another.
The second reaction is to
Strike back at the love partner.
        Why is he so demanding?
        When did his role change from lover to dictator?

If every love is a small dictatorship within the kingdom of one's self,
What right has he to usurp our authority over ourselves?
What right has he to make demands that are not fun to fill?

The bad times begin when the telephone calls are an irritation,
                                not a comfort.
The bad times begin when the things he likes best are the things
                                you like least.
And like so much else in the love relationship,
The bad times have nothing to do with how good the sex is,
For bad times can begin when sex has never been better.

See why we need Lovetalk?
Not for the good times,
But to plug the bad times.
Oh, my dear, bad times are very bad
When the echo of Lovetalk
Does not bring us back to life
And love.

Of what are echoes made?

The ritual of love.

> That's a nice first thing.
> The ritual of love fills deep emotional needs for me.
> I suppose there are a lot of men watching football in
> front of TV sets who don't know that. Instead they know
> who is in the backfield. That is another kind of ritual, but
> it doesn't do much for my kind of love.

The freeing of ourselves from self-preoccupation.

> We get so involved in our own hangnails we neglect to see
> the world is bleeding. Looking up and out makes me hurt
> less, and it is nice for love, too.

Talking, just talking.

> Exploring subjects and ideas is a way to bring bodies and
> minds into harmony. We have to remember talk is not an
> end in itself; it is just a means for getting where our love
> has to go.

Sometimes Lovetalk sounds like such a pretentious way of life,
But it is really a blue jeans approach to love.
I get so sick of seeing people equating glamour with appeal,
Or company manners with courtesy in marriage.
I know you can please and thank you a marriage right into
divorce court,
Because if you can't say what hurts, and I won't stop to listen,
Who's left to tell it to except a couple of attorneys and a judge?

It's really kind of crazy, but Lovetalk doesn't even have to
be of our own making;
Lovetalk can walk into our cluttered lives in somebody else's
words that we apply to our own love. . . .

. . . like the day on the plane when

The stewardess passed the warm, wet towels,
And the woman across the aisle took hers
To gently rub her husband's neck.
I watched and smiled,
And the woman smiled back at me.
          It was a nice, middle-aged, lines-around-the-eyes smile.

I turned my ring 'round and 'round
To say, I understand
What you just said to him.

What is it about fresh love
            that infects me? I just called
            a girl who is new in love, and I asked her
            about him. The phone fizzed gently
            in my hand.

Can't we, who hang our loves upon the wall
            like ancestral portraits, generate enthusiasm,
            too? Didn't we all feel like this once?
            And if once was so good, what's wrong with twice?
            Why don't we rerun the good footage instead of
            replaying the bad?

Back to the telephone.
            "What are you doing for your love?" I asked.
            And she told me about the poems she sent him
            and the funny little cards. She typed his
            speeches and wrote to him every day when he
            was away. "I was afraid he might feel pressured,"
            and a small wistful sound crept into her voice, "so
            I told him if I got too close he should yell. The
            other day he told me I'm possessive. I told him
            he must like it; he didn't yell."

That's because possessive is good.
It's jealous that is bad.
Another day. Another lesson.
And so it goes.

I first knew her husband in business
So when I met her it seemed sort of natural to say
How bright I thought he was.
> Is he? she asked.
> Then she answered herself—
> I suppose in business he is.

I don't mean to be all-knowing . . . but
In business they all are.
For two men live in every man.
Few women know them both;
He shows the world the public man and saves
The private husband just for her.

The private husband who cannot pick up towels or dump garbage.
The non-public he who eats dinner at record speed, falls asleep
> in a chair, and gets up in time to go to bed:
The off-stage executive who nods, grunts, and gives his wife
> world-shaking opinions in monosyllabic monotones.

But then, how dynamic is any bandy-legged,
> thin-haired,
> thick-middled
Forty-year-old once he steps out of his London-cut clothes?

Sometimes when I pick up towels while he sleeps on the sofa
I wonder what
Mrs. Nixon and Mrs. General Motors and Mrs. Paul Newman
Say when the media look the other way.

If you were
To come to me and say
I need you
       I know now
       I would not say

I'm busy.
       It is harder to restart
       Lovetalk than to start it.

       A responsive heart
       A responsive mind
       Make responsive words.

       In response we cradle
       the first sweet words of love.

But first sweet things
—the things that look so easy—
Are the most difficult things in life:

> A line that writes itself,
> A beautiful woman,
> A homemade dinner,
> Creative Lovetalk.

Creative   Creative

✳

A creative act brings order out of chaos
and connects all life

✳

Creative   Creative

✳

Everything is creative now. That's a hot word.
Hot, the way synergistic was two years ago.
I guess creative was a hot word then, too. Still is.
Maybe that's because nobody ever finishes being creative.
You cannot use up creative like a bottle of scotch or
                          last night's roast beef.

So we all keep trying to be creative. Hot stuff.
But how can we make creative Lovetalk?

1. I can be more curious about you.
        You can be more curious about me.

Not just dumb little "what did you do todays," but
really curious. Why do you want the promotion? Is it
for you? Me? Us? How much is ego? Is your ego getting
in the way of your self?
Let's be curious curious, not just dumb-question
boring-answer curious.

2. I can be more concerned about your comforts and interests.
You can have more regard for mine, too. If you hate
what's-her-name, why didn't I refuse her party? And
can't I still? If I could scream every time a football
game comes on TV, then shouldn't you watch
where I can't hear?

3. Balance those crazy old paradoxes . . . that scale of 1 to 10 thing.
Make the needle stay around five. Ouch. Sometimes I get
stabbed by the needle. Quel paradox.

4. Learn the value of separation.
It is not good to be together constantly.
I have a hard time spending all the time with me,
let alone you.
I can make apart time richer. See a movie. Read a book.
Write. Talk to somebody who makes me laugh a lot. I'll
feel better about coming back to you.
I'll like coming home.

Yes. I'll like coming home.

The painting from New York
        that took eight months to frame,
The table quarried from some rock
        two hundred miles from here,
The bibelot a rich man
        once gave our little son,
The china box from friends
        who came to visit us,
The bottle and the mugs
        that you found in Switzerland,
The shelves of books
        we picked with so much thought and care . . .

        They speak our love to me
        Each time I turn the key
        And walk once more into
        The museum of our life.

8

Notes on love (Lovenotes)

I suppose for every man who thinks love is patient acquiescence
        to his every whim,
There is a woman offering patient acquiescence
        and little else.
But can love thrive when one makes rules
        and the other follows them?
I think love is a game with no rulebook.
You win a few, you lose a few,
And you better know how to win without irritating the other person
        and you better know how to lose without crying.

Sometimes it is Lovetalk to say no.
I do not want to yes a man to death,
        but if I did I think I could bring him back to life
        with a well-placed no.
I suppose there are still some mothers who tell their wide-eyed
        virginal daughters that
        no woman can ever say no to her husband,
        or he will seek another woman.
What rot.
The woman who says yes and offers her body with the same fervor
        she hands over her car keys
        should have said no.
Love in a plain brown paper wrapper does not deserve to be opened.

A woman simply cannot be a yes machine
            or she will become a human machine,
            desexed and unloving.
A man, who like some long-forgotten comic character
            smiles and nods "Yes dear"
            may satisfy the teacher instincts in his wife
            but never find the man-woman relationship
            they both require
            for love.

Some people get so involved in marriage they forget about love.
They are so busy making Sunday calls on parents and sending
                  wedding presents to long-distance cousins
That they ignore the short distance from him to her.

That could happen to us very easily.
I kind of like my life
And I confess that there are days
When the institution is preferable to the people.

Love is education in satisfying another's needs.

We are all so damned alone in this overpopulated world
That it is hard to make Lovetalk.
But we can try. We can try.

Love is a specialty that works best in the lives of generalists.

Disaster forces people to examine their loves.
Oh, my dear, why must we wait for disaster?

Many marriages look like patent leather shoes,
Shiny on the outside but sure to crack with use.

It is really a lot easier to let somebody else create our love
                              experiences;
Write our songs, make our movies, tell our stories.
I guess the best reason for creating our own experiences
Is to help us develop the skills for expressing love.
Once we learn the skills, we use them.
Like ice skating, you know.

Some people think it is dangerous, very dangerous, to put emotions
                                        into words.
(Fathers tell that to their sons very early in the game.
Mothers tell it to their daughters as one of the facts of life.)
Maybe we distrust words,
Because deceit and falsehood are practiced more by words than deeds.
Yet words are important in giving form to thought.
Nothing is so unless we say it is so.
If we instinctively think something to be so,
            that does not make it so.

Only words bring ideas to life.
And love is but one good idea. . . .
Can we afford not to beget each good idea that we can?
Speak . . . love . . . talk . . . love . . . lovetalk . . . talk love.

If through Lovetalk
We can right the wrongs between us
Then we are but one step
From seeing the injustices about us
And speaking out
To right the human state.

✻

Now.

✻

While there is still some time.

She telephoned today.
My friend, the widow, telephoned today.
It was such a good marriage.
Good solid strong interdependent marriage.
"I did not know how much I needed him," she cried to me.
"I sit here now in pants and sweater, scarf and shoes.
Only the shoes did I buy. All the other things he bought for me.
Yet he was not an easy man.
When he died, my son said . . . with you he had thirty years of bliss.
He could not have had one good year with any other woman.
But for me they were thirty years of bliss, too.
This house is so sad I must get out of it.
I must leave the table he made and the flowers he planted.
I am miserable. You cannot know how miserable this is."

Yes, I can, dear friend. Yes I can.
Must I be blind to know a sightless world?
Must I die to know what living is?
I can feel for you. I can feel, for
The time must never come when I cannot feel
For those I know.
For if it does,
I will not feel for me.

I cannot dry your tears,
But I can feel them.
I can feel them.

I saw the out-of-town executive at a meeting the other day
And he pulled out the pictures of the blond, smiling kids
And I looked and said, "They're adorable. When did you last see
                    them?"
He shuffled the pictures like playing cards, put them back in his
                    wallet and smiled.
"Funny you should ask," he said with that nervous laugh that reduces
                    executives to human levels,
"But last week when I was running a sales meeting in Los Angeles,
                    my wife called and said . . .
'Maybe you'll be president of the world someday, but you won't be
                    my husband' . . .
I got on the next plane and went home for a week."

I wonder if he thinks he saved his marriage with one flying leap.
I doubt it. I don't think that's Lovetalk.
I mean, how loving can it be when she threatens and he runs?
Somehow or other I think it would have meant more if he had picked
                    up the telephone
To call home and had said, "I don't care if I'm president of the
                    world someday
    Just so long as I can be your husband everyday." . . .
And then he should have flown home for a week.
I happen to think that women in their loving little heads
                    would rather be treated like women
Than long-forgotten disciplinarians. Home just shouldn't be
                    the principal's office.

94

I met a psychiatrist, and he said
He didn't think people should get married
In order to help each other.
He believed a woman should be her husband's wife
And not his psychiatrist.
He said people should first be whole
And then get married.
Then he turned to me and said, "What do you think?"
Oh, you nice sweet dear psychiatrist.
How kind that you should care what I think,
But how can I give you a quick answer when
I have spent my whole life trying to find out what I think?

A reporter wanted to interview me, so he came to breakfast with my daughter and me. He told us about the girl he loved and the poetry he wrote, and he seemed so full of love and the need to marry this girl that I responded with several knowing clucks and sympathetic sighs.

When he left, I said to my daughter, "People tell me so many things. They think I have all the answers, but I don't."

My daughter looked at me soberly. "That's right," she said, "you don't."

O